Praise for *The Origin of the Milky Way*

"Barbara Ungar's new book is a departure: her earlier work was all about the joy, the sudden access of energy she pulled from 'the used, the worn, the broken in.' This book is about giving birth out of one's own body to another body. She confronts the exhilarations and terrors (as well as, she fears, sweet delusions) of birth frontally, even ruthlessly. The unit here is mother and son. As soon as she is pregnant, for the speaker the father ceases to exist. This is a compelling mirror." —Frank Bidart

"Barbara Louise Ungar's *The Origin of the Milky Way* is a fearless, unflinching collection about birth and motherhood, the transformation of bodies. Ungar's poems are honestly brutal, candidly tender. Their primal immediacy and intense intimacy are realized through her dazzling sense of craft. Ungar delivers a wonderful, sensuous, visceral poetry." —Denise Duhamel, author of *Two and Two*, winner of the 2007 Milt Kessler Poetry Book Award

"Ungar's mesoblastic poetry refreshes the tattered Modern Soul!" —Sparrow, author of *Yes, You ARE a Revolutionary!*

"The theme of motherhood has inspired many of the worst and only a handful of the best contemporary poems, but Barbara Ungar's book of variations on that theme explores it with a dazzling range of accents. By turns witty and euphoric, panic-stricken and exalted, Ungar does comedy and rage, tenderness and meditation in poems consistently inventive and intelligent." —Peg Boyers, editor of *Salmagundi* and author of *Honey with Tobacco*

"Evocative and skillfully crafted, Barbara Louise Ungar's *The Origin of the Milky Way* succeeds in revealing the connectedness of each of us in an expanding universe through poems of creation, birth, and maternity. Inventive and sometimes playful, Ungar's verse exhibits a passion for a clean line and precise diction. Poems in this compelling collection are highly accessible and transportive. From the very first poem, "Embryology," the reader is pulled into the magical and heady experience of conception. And one suddenly becomes keenly aware that the title of this collection reflects on far more than the galaxy containing our own solar system. In the beautifully rendered title poem, "In Tintoretto's *The Origin of the Milky Way*," an ekphrastic poem in response to a painting in which Jupiter holds the infant Hercules to the breast of Juno, Ungar notes, "All the faces, even her mask / of perfection, gaze toward that miracle / of milk." Ungar's fresh and multilayered poems thematically invoke creation, mythology, alchemy, religion, and even rock 'n' roll as they move from conception through the prepartum, parturient, and postpartum periods to a mindfulness of middle age and matronhood. Whether delicate or hard-edged, these poems resonate in a cohesive collection. Ungar has touched on something vital to all of us—"in the last, we grow and do not know / how or who is holding us, yet we are held." —Donna J. Gelagotis Lee, judge of the 2006 Gival Press Poetry Award and author of *On the Altar of Greece*

4/25/2009

Saratoga

The

Origin

of the

Milky Way

For Helena ~

Barbara Louise Ungar

With gratitude

& joy ~

Barbara

Arlington, Virginia

Published by Gival Press, an imprint of Gival Press, LLC.

For information please write:

Gival Press, LLC, P. O. Box 3812, Arlington, VA 22203.

Website: *www.givalpress.com*

Email: *givalpress@yahoo.com*

First edition ISBN 13: 978-1-928589-39-6

Library of Congress Control Number: 2007935326

Book cover artwork: "The Origin of the Milky Way" Jacopo Tintoretto Bought, 1890 Credit: © The National Gallery, London.

Book Format and design by Ken Schellenberg.

Photo of Barbara Louise Ungar by Beth DellaRocco.

Acknowledgements

"News," *Salmagundi*, Fall 2007.

"Embryology," Center for Book Arts broadside, November 2003.

"Matryoshka," "Countdown," and "Prepartum Blues," *Glens Falls Post Star*, 2005.

"Prepartum Blues," *Metroland*, Albany, New York, 2004.

"Embryology," "Ultrasonics," "Riddle," "Prenatal Yoga," "Quickening," "Dream at Twenty-Three Weeks," "Matryoshka," "Threshold," "Annunciations," "Alchemy at Nine Months," "Uroboros," "Prepartum Blues," "Coup," "Countdown," "Labor," "Transference," "After Birth," "Fourth Trimester," "Be My Baby," "Deerwood, Minnesota," "Why They're Called the Wee Hours," "Madonna and Child," "Izaak Laughing," "Simple," and "Ark" appeared in the chapbook, *Sequel*, Finishing Line Press, 2004. Reprinted by permission of Finishing Line Press.

Eternal gratitude to my teachers, Frank Bidart, Ann Lauterbach, and Angus Fletcher, and to the Poetry Doctors, Stuart Bartow and Naton Leslie. Many, many thanks to Paul Elisha, Ba Kaiser, Joe Kraussman, Sue Oringel, Ann Settel, Sara Wiest, and all the members of Frank's Poetry Factory, especially Peg Boyers, Lee Gould, Eva Hooker, Louise Katz, and Julie Suarez. Special thanks to Beth DellaRocco and Denise Duhamel. Thanks above all to Izaak for giving me the inspiration and occasions for these poems. Grateful thanks to the College of Saint Rose for giving me sabbatical and release time to write them.

Contents

I. Annunciations

II. Liminal

III. Fourth Trimester

IV. Feast

for Izaak

I. Annunciations

Embryology

Could it just be hormones,
this euphoria
as if someone rubbed petals

of opium poppy all over
me, inside and out,
or could it be true

what the rabbis say:
when sperm meets egg
two angels enter to teach

the soul that floats,
growing, in darkness—
one angel holds a candle

so the new being can see
to the end of the universe
and back

and when lessons are through,
one angel taps
three times the upper lip

and departs
as the babe, in travail,
fights its way into *The vale*

of Soul-making alone,
and marked,
having forgotten everything.

Ultrasonics

The way fishermen find shoals
of deep-sea fish and navies track
submarines, the way bats
net moths, barnstorming the darkness,
or dolphins and whales echolocate
their worlds, bouncing high-
pitched sounds from melon-foreheads
and back through their receiving jaws,

the way I first saw you, bowled fish,
wingless bat, lost submariner, bumping
blind in my belly like some mini-Jonah,
a mere inch, the coming one, who
will be heaved out on dry land
from the ocean's maw.

Riddle

There's a penis deep inside me,
   getting bigger every day.

I'm growing balls
   & big teats at once.

I'm of two minds, two mouths,
   four thumbs.

I've got a pair
   of hearts.

Twenty toes &
   twenty perfect toenails.

Hair up & down,
   & lanugo to boot.

One womb, one way
   in & out—the hard strait

he'll have to take.

Quickening

A butterfly wing
  brushes you inside—

A liquid hiccup?
  A whisper:

There's some
  body else

in here
  with you.

Prenatal Yoga

Every body here has two hearts
    except the teacher.

In a circle we sit and
    stolidly glow.

We say our names, what
    we do, when

we're due—a calendar
    of ripening.

We practice breathing
    into our backs.

We practice opening
    wide as the ocean.

Soon we will be tested,
    like billions before us, bitches

and bugs, driven to the edge
    where something

comes out of nothing,
    a piece of ourselves

splits off from us,
    godcund. Each

zooms past the speed of light
   toward the center

of her own Milky Way—
   that single point

dense as millions of suns,
   roar of star formation—

Your spine is a river of light
   the teacher says.

Let your heart bow
   to your baby's heart.

Dream at Twenty-three Weeks

I've given birth to a frog,
only two inches long.
I adore him. He's a genius,

a talking frog. Very quick,
he hops into the closet
but I nab him. He leaps out

the car door; I jump after
& grab him. He hops
away, but I hold on:

his back leg, stuck, stretches
& stretches till his foot
comes off. I put it on my left breast:

We have to get him to a vet right away.
His little green foot
falls off. Frantic, I think

What a terrible mother I am.

Matryoshka

You move in me as I
in earth's strange atmosphere,

as her blue-green ball spins in the expanding darkness—

within me, you cannot fathom me,
as I can't see the globe I tread, but feel her

warmth, her motions rocking me

to sleep, her rest in which I wake, and she
never dreams in whose body she sleeps, turning—

like Matryoshka dolls, the next nesting

in the last, we grow and do not know
how or who is holding us, yet we are held.

Threshold

I've become a door.
Someone's knocking.

I'll swing open
once for the guest

to come in.
Then shut.

I'll grow trans-
parent and slide

away, the limen
between here

and where
we come from

and go.

Annunciations

That line of golden script

from Gabriel's mouth to her ear—
she turns inward, tuned solely

to sound that is not sound

but seismic wave in water, ultra sound,
as bats' exquisitely sensitive ears

flap shut a hundred times a second

so as not to be deafened
by their own sonar shrieks. A mother

bat picks out her baby's squeak

in a cave hung with hordes. So I wake
at your faintest cry, already tuned

to silent signal, minute ripple within.

I do not comprehend—(*my body
is making another body*)—any more than

how to pack an amaryllis in its bulb
or unfurl its astonishing red trumpets.

The word has pierced my ear.

Alchemy at Nine Months

Have I swallowed the philosopher's
stone? An alembic

wherein strange matters burble,
like a lava lamp. O elixir!

I'm turning dross to gold. Like
Rumplestiltskin's queen, I sit

spinning, worrying over names.
Or a jumbo jet, hold

heaped with cargo, taxiing till my turn
to lumber aloft, solo pilot

unseen at the inscrutable controls.

Uroboros

No more tadpole or darting fish—
when you move now, the slow coils
of a python rearrange their knot

as my belly undulates—
Uroboros—serpent or dragon
devouring its tail: soon

your mouth will emerge
from between my legs
and begin to suck,

making us one mobius strip,
my inside turning in-
to your outside, seamlessly.

Prepartum Blues

I miss you
and you're not even born yet.

How sad when you're outside
and I'm an empty barn.

I'll miss this lively dancing.

Already you elude me, squirming
toward the world of shapes and loss.

Bulb in the dirt, head-
long for the light,

you'll pierce and leave
me behind, some darkness

clinging to your shadow.

Bulb. Tuber. Root
in the cellar. Mole. Blind
burrower. Tunneler in my yard.

Coup

My brain is abandoning me,
curling up in a corner
of its skull, a hibernating
squirrel. I stumble
like a zombie, spill, trip,
drop, bump, fall, forget.

My uterus, swollen with power,
has taken over Central Command:
on auto-pilot, bones loosen, ligaments
go soft, hormones flood, all systems
on count-down
to blast-off. The womb

has done this zillions of times,
once for every creature made since Eve:
Squirrel-brain-and-Zombie-I can only
hunker down harder, roll sleepily
out of its way—the Juggernaut,
the Great Beast, Mother of us all.

Countdown

Each day I think,
*This could be my last day
alone
for the rest of my life—*

What have I done?

I who love solitude
above all things

will soon love
something more —
Some one
I have never met—

What have I done?

II. Liminal

Blanche's Tale

I'm looking forward to becoming a *great-*
grandmother. But I remember how scared
I was of giving birth. I was six months
pregnant. We were living upstairs,
in a four-plex. The woman downstairs
was *very* pregnant. One day her nine-year-old girl
knocked on the door and said to Leon,

> *Mom needs your help.*

He put on his coat to drive her to the hospital.
When I didn't see any car, I went down
to check. The back door was opposite the bathroom;
there she was sitting on the toilet, with Leon
standing next to her. The other downstairs neighbor
was at the kitchen table reading out loud
from a medical text.

> *Something's happening,*

the woman said. I pushed Leon aside
and saw the sac in the toilet. He reached down
just in time to catch the baby.
She got up and lit a cigarette, stood there
smoking, still attached.
She had not felt one pain.
Just then the milkman showed up
at the back door and said,

How many bottles?

No milk today,

she said. Later, a doctor
came and cut the cord, an ambulance
took them to the hospital. After that,
all my fear was gone.

Labor

No one tells you—
how could they?

They could say
it was like being
drawn and quartered,
—not once,
with death as respite,
but, as in the *Inferno*,
reconstituted
only to be rent again,
twenty, then thirty
times an hour,
with increasing violence.
(Dante, had he watched,
would have fainted.) Or
the perfect engine
of the Inquisition,
inserted
to be opened
and opened till
you're torn apart. Or
crushed
to a single unbearable
point, microcosmos
at the moment of Big Bang—
and the only way out
is to blow yourself apart.

None of these
comes near it.

How does anyone
do it twice?

They say
you forget.

This is to make sure
I don't.

Transference

How many women fall in love
with their obstetrician? Who could forget
his hand on her arm at his arrival—Orpheus

touching Eurydice in Hell—that music
in its stroke down her forearm.
Does my doctor know

his patients adore him? He sees the unseen
parts of us. How many lovers ever praised
your cervix, that pink-glazed donut?

His small hands travel where no
others do (inside the donut hole)
while your husband turns away.

Could his wife suspect we debate whether
to murder or include her in our harem?
What would it be like to have your husband

out most nights with other women,
coming home at all hours
exhausted and smelling of afterbirth?

After Birth

The doctor, her father, sits sniffing his hands:

Come smell

the most wonderful smell in the world.

Ten years old, suspicious:

What is it?

Afterbirth.

Now she wonders what she missed.
Essential oil of newborn heads? *Eau de l'autre côté,*
scent of heaven or wherever we come from,

perfume that makes women melt,
ineffable as the fragrance of snow—
essence of creation emanating

out the open skull? It fades
slowly as the soft spot closes up like the last
patch of dark water in a freezing lake.

III. Fourth Trimester

Fourth Trimester

You fit in-
to the crook
of my body with
the satisfying
click
of the last
blue-sky piece
of jigsaw
puzzled over
for months
only
on the out-
side now.

Be My Baby

We were born in the 50s, when your grandma
didn't breastfeed because *It was too animalistic,*
when animal was bad, science good.

They gave you a shot and when you woke up,
you had a baby. Before rock 'n' roll
made animal good. Nursing,

you grunt and squeal like James Brown,
plump as Elvis bursting out of your powderblue
jumpsuit. Your hands like Joe Cocker's

pluck notes out of mid-air, dance like Jagger's
around the mike. You rest one foot
on my thigh, nonchalant as James Dean,

cool as Brando chatting up some girl
with a foot on the curb (cigarette
tucked in your onesie sleeve). Your arm

windmills and thwacks my breast
like Pete Townshend's guitar. They all
imitated you: the great ones

never lose their infantine
grace, their mainline to pure
desire and release: Marvin Gaye

wheeled onstage on a couch, supine
and crooning. Bliss when you latch on,
rage when you can't, the roots of rock 'n' roll.

Just add three chords, Bo Diddly said.
You can't sing yet, duckwalk or play guitar, but
baby, when you cry, you break your mama's heart.

Deerwood, Minnesota

5:30 a.m. The loons cry
four times, slicing
the quiet circle of the lake.

I'm half-awake, in the long swoon of nursing.

Six loons live on the lake
this summer, two pair
with one baby each. Rare.

Though this world trembles on the brink
of extinction, the lake still
brims with laughter, great northern divers

dance on the water in their checkered necklaces.

I heard you talking in a dream
and surfaced to find you calling me,
still wordless,

as the embergoslings also call.

Why They're Called The Wee Hours

No one's awake but
baby & me
& the man who drives the snow
plow & the baker &
deliveryman   longdistance truckers
allnight poets
pilots & their crews
the night shift   nocturnal creatures
stuffed animals come to life
& billions of people on the side
of the world closer to the sun

But it's just you & me
& the man who drives the snowplow
here on our street in this still
cold dark hour   the changing
table lit by his eerie orange
strobe   He gets up in the middle
of the night while half the world breathes
snuginitswarmbed & puts on boots
struggles out into the storm
to make the street safe

What a way to make a living
and yet   there is purity
in service: how good to exist
for someone else, to leave
your comfort behind—
a simple job unseen
backbreaking constant
changing the snowy
diaper of the street

Crying

Why is it so hard when you
won't stop, can't
be comforted? My own

tears unheeded, left
alone in a room to wail
and learn no one would come

till I stopped crying
entirely, stopped expecting
anyone would ever come.

I swore I'd never do that to you
but sometimes I step on a landmine
of rage and have to put you

down. Grownups
can shake their babies like rattles
when they can't bear the grating

pain unattended all these years,
the baby's shriek an electric
can opener slicing

the skull of worms.
This world hurts. If I wanted
to spare you, I should never

have brought you here.
Your crying flays me,
peels the sleepless lids,

exposes my innards
like The Visible Woman's—
every nerve raw and muscle

clenched—even after
you hush and drop off,
exhausted angel, I think

I hear you in the house's moaning.

Nursing Hunger

Suddenly ravening, a famine-panic
as the body turns on itself—
not just starving, but hounded

as if by lust, the Great Bitch
clawing through your flimsy shape—
why, if you trip and fall,

your reflexes, rewired,
protect your cub now, not yourself—
your very flesh would gladly

deliquesce, if necessary, pool
every cell into milk, leaving you
a pale puddle on the cave's dark floor.

Postpartum Blues

I've had four hours of sleep.
My head aches. I slipped
on the ice & sprained my knee.
I'm reduced to formula in my coffee.

You won't go down, you're heavy,
if you're not in my arms, you scream,
more beautiful than sunlight
in your butteryellow outfit.

Multiply by two,
add a cheating love, then
frozen pipes: now you know
why Sylvia stuck her head in the oven.

Tanka

Horses stand in the rain
head down in an open field.
What else can they do?

It's not labor.
I can stand it.

Nap

I fold you back in
to my softdark
warmrocking till we blur
past the border no one's ever
seen and I too am wrapped
back up in the exhaling
darkness that feeds us

Pool

The last time I swam here, I didn't know
my water had broken.
You were on your last lap—no,

stuck in the middle of a flip-

turn, head wedged
between my hips
so I waddled like a goose

stuffed and tethered for *foie gras*.

When I lowered in my gravid bod
and pushed off, merganser-graceful,
I could no longer flutter-kick, just frog.

No comfort but in water.

At last I hauled our ponderousness
up   each   step,   like an astronaut
re-entering gravity's crush.

In the parking lot, the first pains.

Breathe out, breathe in, follow the dark
line down the center of the lane
toward the deep

end, a violet blur.

Simple

All craving in your gaping mouth
    and grasping hands,

satisfaction in the nipple's
    target—

Bullseye. Perfect union.
    Like sex, only simpler.

After the endless night, the dark
    night of separate rooms,

we are one again,
    latched on to the light.

You don't know yet.
    And I forget:

Each breath a sip of
    the universe,

each bite a mouthful
    of earth and star.

IV. Feast

Izaak Laughing

I named you for laughter.
Yitzhak, to laugh. In morning sun
I read the paper and sip tea
while you chase Zooey
the cat and practice your laugh.

In Africa, *The horror*—
the horror—in Schenectady
Jeffrey Skinner beat
three-month-old Samantha Rio to death.

You pull yesterday's horrors from the rack,
shred them, stuff some in your mouth
and work like cud. You sit
so beautifully, upright and plumb,
smiling young Buddha
who eats all suffering.

Proprioception

You surf the rolling
earth in your new
mouse-shoes with elastic
whiskers, your tai chi
arms fluid on air, open-
mouthed, ecstatic.

Ride the bucking
planet, fling your hat
off, crowing, throw
yourself off-
balance with pride, clamber
up and try again.

And again. First,
to sit. Soon, to walk,
ride a bike, skateboard,
tank. Relentless
drive. Fearlessness.
Falling and falling and falling.

Icon

You strive to be a vessel of light
and love for the miraculous

shoved out through your dark body—

Here it is, nonstop:
trouble, sleepless care, shit and blood and wailing

inconsolable—till you snap

and yell—shades of the prison-
house, your own Iron Mom.

And again you vow endless patience,

to be mild as the Blessèd Mother
you don't believe in. Those terrible icons:

perfect virgin and magical son;

the broken sac of bones
he will become

when time and men have done with him;

the open, empty, upturned
hands of the mother

who has survived her child.

Prelude

Once I gave birth I was sentenced to grieve
over the wild fear that you could be torn
from my arms. Rent garment, smeared ash, or shorn
hair—nothing could blunt my keen bereavement,
should I be forced to wake to a morning
when you are not. How far beyond forlorn
would I dwell, if I survived. Imagine Eve
after Abel dropped. The first death. To leave

Eden was but prelude to that loss. Within
herself, bearing exile wherever she went,
she ached for him, growing hollow and thin
as any soldier's mother, having spent
years of night contending with God: What sin
(Old bloody Father) could deserve such banishment?

News

He just squirmed away from you in the tub, his perfect, slippery body . . . You'd think, from the TV, that they don't love their kids the way we do. I read about one mother whose son had blown himself up, taking others with him, as he'd been taught was good. She said: *If I had known, I would have taken an ax and hacked open my chest and sewed him into my heart where he would be safe.*

Mine

We learn possessives. Possession.
To be possessed: *MINE. Mommy tea.*

Daddy car. He'll snatch a curling iron
from his sister's hand, *MINE.*

Carry it around for days,
tripping over the cord. *MINE.*

Halt on daycare stairs to announce,
belligerent: *Dis MINE.*

What one wants, all want:
some green plastic bowl

becomes the holy grail they take turns
taking home at night. They play

tug-of-war with the curling iron
in the fallen leaves. I wish

my boy never to be a soldier.
There is no end to war, says Li Po. War,

from the Sanskrit: *The desire for more cows.*

Armistice Day

Reading the names of the dead
outside in November wind
fingers numb   no one stops
all hurry past   hands shoved in pockets
heads down against the blast
dry leaves skitter on concrete
sere November polish on the world
thin sun glitters through newly stripped
trees   on gold and brown leaves and silver
pampas grass   Persephone descends
the stairs
        Try to feel for each
mother   give each ghost
one breath   inhabit peripherally
age   rank   manner of death
begin to say the hometowns too
to anchor each name to some spot
as the wires stuck through white
paper flags flapping on the green
pin each name to the earth
till torn loose they will fly
off like leaves

When will we force those powermad
old men to wrestle naked in the mud
to the death instead

Madonna and Child

The Marys fare better, probably
the various wives and lovers
of painters glad to have a good
pious excuse for an exposed
breast—their variously beautiful
faces drenched in love—

Every painter a Joseph
outside the golden circle
looking in, suspecting
he's not really the father,
shut out from the sacred
transaction between
mother and child, palpable
in their entranced gaze.

The boy sometimes holds a ball,
the world, as infants do,
in curiously adult hands,
enthroned, omnipotent.

Those grotesque baby-
sized men in their mamas' laps.

Men can recognize divinity
in women, in infants barely,
most rarely in each other. The babe

must grow to be betrayed,
abandoned, left to die, broken
in his weeping mama's lap.
*Every mother knows
her god.*

Like a Faucet

When it wakes you, insistent, in the middle
of the night, your husband's penis is one more
baby demanding to be stroked & rocked,
one more mouth to soothe & feed
& clean up after.

Your desire now is to be inviolate,
not this public square where everyone
transacts, this service station where the family
fills up, but to sleep uninterrupted
as virgin beach.

Alas, those arrangements that once enraged you
(European marriages, Chinese concubines)
now appear as relief. Have you travelled
beyond jealousy so far? And who is this stranger
that occupies your bed?

Poor man, fallen from God-the-Father
to baby-in-waiting: He can't compete
with his fragrant avatar. You'd trade every
orgasm, that string of glass beads, for the New
World of infant smiles.

You are in love, again and for the first time,
thinking, this love can never be diverted, turn
cold, or off.

Becoming a Virgin

They say Aphrodite (yes, She

who wore the golden girdle
men found irresistable, who cuckolded
her lame and ugly hubby every chance

she got) renewed her virginity
simply by bathing
in the blue sea at Paphos.

Her priestess, too, immersed
every spring in Cyprian
water, emerged virgin.

Myth any stranger than fact?

This elastic body
grew a second body
inside, spewed it forth, then sprang

back to (almost) its former shape.
Now I long to fly
in a car drawn by sparrows and doves

to that rocky coast
to plunge into bracing salt
to rise closed.

To Women of A Certain Age

Weep, mommies. Weep
for hard bodies, wet
lips, petal cheeks—
weep for the tight buds
fragrant with unspilled perfume,
for the blown rose made lace
by rapacious beetles.

Having squeezed out your
perfect fruit, your petals
droop toward decay. Why
entertain the bee again?

Watch your daughter sail blithely
into the cloud of fucking
as you stumble out the other side,
shaking your dyed, greying locks,
going, *What was that?*

What leviathan rolled you
thirty years in his ocean bed?

Look, the sober knitting
of matronhood proves
as essential to the wedding
as that your daughter dance.

Weep, mommies, nymphs no more,
for the world that chases nymphs
tirelessly as Zeus, while you
haul the water and wring the sheets,
beast of love's burden. Love
has transformed you as utterly
as if you had grown bark—
no heads swivel in the street, the wolf
whistles only for your daughter,
and though you have even less
interest in them than they in you, this
somehow hurts.

        See?
            Night coming, and you
one cell in her vast body.

My Teen Muse ODs on Heroin

I. Before

*You could pretend I died & write a poem
about me*, suggests my sultry muse,
my spiritual daughter. The one I wrote
yesterday's not enough. Insatiable
for praise as any artist. Death's unreal,
pure play to her, immortal teenager.

No more to her than the mite's demise
to my toddler son, who squeals with delight,
BUG! His thumb descends on the highchair
tray, haphazard, the way of gods.

No make-believe. Since his birth, I dissolve
at the merest pinch of death. *We have no time
alone together anymore*, my teen muse whines.
And he cries. *We should give him up for adoption.*

II. After

Cassandra lies. We all believe her.
When she tells the truth, no one can.
An actress, she blurs the difference,
finds lotus to ease the grief. No use
telling her how ancient her story is,
how inescapable: she won't believe you.

All teenagers think they're invincible

they tell you in rehab, *but Cassie*
thinks she's more invincible than most.
Not every girl gets chased by a god
and has got the moxie to blow him off.

We think we know her end. Locked in her curse
she refuses to cry: spun round in time,
to recall the future, she blacks out the past.

Why There Aren't More Poems About Toddlers

Where's the paper? Where
are all the pens? Where are my
scrawled ideas for poems?
Where has my dream journal fled?

The baby eats erasers and draws
on walls, scribbles in library books,
loses pen caps, scatters scratch
paper, flushes pencils
to catch paper till the toilet chokes
after you've dumped a diaper in
(a repeating dream you no longer bother to analyze).

Because the naked two-year-old
squealing under your bed
has the plunger; because while you shower
he microwaves potholders, salts the teapot,
peppers the sofa, pours milk on rugs;
because he's magnetized by knives
scissors water & electricity.

Because, with luck, he will leave
for school and break your heart.
And still you'll wonder, where
did it all go?

In Tintoretto's *Origin of the Milky Way*,

Jupiter coasts in, tailed by his eagle,
thrusting baby Hercules out toward Juno's
breast. She sprawls diagonally

naked across the painting's center,
her luxe Venetian bed entangled in clouds.
Four cherubim zoom in with bow and arrows,

chains and net; her peacocks watch. Shining rays
spray from her nipples: the right streaming
down to plant lilies in earth; the left

shooting up—past the bastard infant's head
and her bangled arm upflung into sky—
to flower in ten golden stars.

All the faces, even her mask
of perfection, gaze toward that miracle
of milk. Startled awake, she leans back, bare

foot treading thundercloud, one hand open
above both their heads (the faithless god's
and some mortal woman's son), as if she,

goddess of childbirth, had just flung
newborn stars. The astonishment of milk
arcing out into space, her stranger body

showering in spontaneous creation.

Feast

After all the parties, all the wine
    the wee hours, one with God
        and dark, goldtipped cigarettes

After trying all the restaurants and drugs
    at least once, the hangovers twice

After dancing all night
    so many nights you've worn out
        not your slippers but your hip

After Bali and Burma
    ecstasy in the Forum
        and windsurfing in Greece

After forty-five years

    to be turned
      into a feast

    to be eaten alive
      and become more alive

    body transmuted
      into perfect food

    to be consumed
      yet not used up

breasts, magic botas

that fill and refill more
      the more they're emptied

to be worn out
      by nine every night

and find no body sweeter than sleep.

Ark

My pelvis a boat
in which you rocked on the dark

waters, carrying
you across, out of nowhere

to here, the unknown
passage, Charon in reverse—

each one of us rocked
in our mama's bone canoe,

a frail line stretching
back to Africa, back to

Ocean, back to Light.

Books Available from Gival Press
Poetry

Bones Washed With Wine: Flint Shards from Sussex and Bliss
by Jeff Mann
 ISBN 13: 978-1-928589-14-3, $15.00
 Includes the 1999 Gival Press Poetry Award winning collection.
 Jeff Mann is "a poet to treasure both for the wealth of his
 language and the generosity of his spirit."
 — Edward Falco, author of *Acid*

Canciones para sola cuerda / Songs for a Single String
by Jesús Gardea; English translation by Robert L. Giron
 ISBN 13: 978-1-928589-09-9, $15.00
 Finalist for the 2003 Violet Crown Book Award—Literary Prose
 & Poetry. Love poems, with echoes of Neruda à la Mexicana,
 Gardea writes about the primeval quest for the perfect woman.

Dervish by Gerard Wozek
 ISBN 13: 978-1-928589-11-2, $15.00
 Winner of the 2000 Gival Press Poetry Award / Finalist for the
 2002 Violet Crown Book Award—Literary Prose & Poetry.
 "By jove, these poems shimmer."
 —Gerry Gomez Pearlberg, author of *Mr. Bluebird*

The Great Canopy by Paula Goldman
 ISBN 13: 1-928589-31-0, $15.00
 Winner of the 2004 Gival Press Poetry Award / 2006
 Independent Publisher Book Award—Honorable Mention for
 Poetry
 "Under this canopy we experience the physicality of the body
 through Goldman's wonderfully muscular verse as well the
 analytics of a mind that tackles the meaning of Orpheus or the
 notion of desire."
 — Richard Jackson, author of *Half Lives*

Let Orpheus Take Your Hand by George Klawitter
 ISBN 13: 978-1-928589-16-7, $15.00
 Winner of the 2001 Gival Press Poetry Award
 A thought provoking work that mixes the spiritual with stealthy
 desire, with Orpheus leading us out of the pit.

Metamorphosis of the Serpent God by Robert L. Giron
ISBN 13: 978-1-928589-07-5, $12.00
This collection "...embraces the past and the present, ethnic and sexual identity, themes both mythical and personal."
—*The Midwest Book Review*

On the Altar of Greece by Donna J. Gelagotis Lee
ISBN 13: 978-1-92-8589-36-5, $15.00
Winner of the 2005 Gival Press Poetry Award / 2007 Eric Hoffer Book Award: Notable for Art Category
"...*On the Altar of Greece* is like a good travel guide: it transforms reader into visitor and nearly into resident. It takes the visitor to the authentic places that few tourists find, places delightful yet still surprising, safe yet unexpected...."
—by Simmons B. Buntin, editor of *Terrain.org* Blog

On the Tongue by Jeff Mann
ISBN 13: 978-1-928589-35-8, $15.00
"...These poems are ...nothing short of extraordinary."
—Trebor Healey, author of *Sweet Son of Pan*

The Nature Sonnets by Jill Williams
ISBN 13: 978-1-928589-10-5, $8.95
An innovative collection of sonnets that speaks to the cycle of nature and life, crafted with wit and clarity. "Refreshing and pleasing."
— Miles David Moore, author of *The Bears of Paris*

The Origin of the Milky Way by Barbara Louise Ungar
ISBN 13: 978-1-928589-39-6, $15.00
Winner of the 2006 Gival Press Poetry Award
"...a fearless, unflinching collection about birth and motherhood, the transformation of bodies. Ungar's poems are honestly brutal, candidly tender. Their primal immediacy and intense intimacy are realized through her dazzling sense of craft. Ungar delivers a wonderful, sensuous, visceral poetry." —Denise Duhamel

Poetic Voices Without Borders edited by Robert L. Giron
ISBN 13: 978-1-928589-30-3, $20.00
2006 Writer's Notes Magazine Book Award—Notable for Art /
2006 Independent Publisher Book Award—Honorable Mention
for Anthology
An international anthology of poetry in English, French, and
Spanish, including work by Grace Cavalieri, Jewell Gomez, Joy
Harjo, Peter Klappert, Jaime Manrique, C.M. Mayo, E. Ethelbert
Miller, Richard Peabody, Myra Sklarew and many others.

Poetic Voices Without Borders 2, edited by Robert L. Giron
ISBN 13: 978-1-928589-43-3, $20.00
Featuring poets Grace Cavalieri, Rita Dove, Dana Gioia, Joy
Harjo, Peter Klappert, Philip Levine, Gloria Vando, and many
other fine poets in English, French, and Spanish.

Prosody in England and Elsewhere:
A Comparative Approach by Leonardo Malcovati
ISBN 13: 978-1-928589-26-6, $20.00
The perfect tool for the poet but written for a non-specialist
audience.

Protection by Gregg Shapiro
ISBN 13: 978-1-928589-41-9, $15.00
"Gregg Shapiro's stunning debut marks the arrival of a new
master poet on the scene. His work blows me away."
—Greg Herren, author of *Mardi Gras Mambo*

Songs for the Spirit by Robert L. Giron
ISBN 13: 978-1-928589-0802, $16.95
A psalter for the reader who is not religious but who is spiritually
inclined. "This is an extraordinary book."
—John Shelby Spong

Sweet to Burn by Beverly Burch
ISBN 13: 978-1-928589-23-5, $15.00
Winner of the 2004 Lambda Literary Award for Lesbian Poetry
Winner of the 2003 Gival Press Poetry Award — "Novelistic in
scope, but packing the emotional intensity of lyric poetry..."
— Eloise Klein Healy, author of *Passing*

Tickets to a Closing Play by Janet I. Buck
ISBN 13: 978-1-928589-25-9, $15.00
Winner of the 2002 Gival Press Poetry Award
"...this rich and vibrant collection of poetry [is] not only serious and insightful, but a sheer delight to read."—Jane Butkin Roth, editor of *We Used to Be Wives: Divorce Unveiled Through Poetry*

Where a Poet Ought Not / Où c'qui faut pas by G. Tod Slone
(in English and French)
ISBN 13: 978-1-928589-42-6, $15.00
Poems inspired by French poets Léo Ferré and François Villon and the Québec poet Raymond Lévesque in what Slone characterizes as a need to speak up. "In other words, a poet should speak the truth as he sees it and fight his damnedest to overcome all the forces encouraging not to."

For a list of poetry published by Gival Press, please visit: *www.givalpress.com.*

Books available via Ingram, the Internet, and other outlets.

Or Write:
Gival Press, LLC
PO Box 3812
Arlington, VA 22203
703.351.0079

Made in the USA